Samuel Menashe

AMERICAN POETS PROJECT

THE NEGLECTED MASTERS AWARD

WAS ESTABLISHED BY

The Poetry Foundation

*and this volume is published in conjunction
with that honor*

———

AMERICAN POETS PROJECT

is published with a gift in memory of

James Merrill

and support from its Founding Patrons

Sidney J. Weinberg, Jr. Foundation

The Berkley Foundation

Richard B. Fisher & Jeanne Donovan Fisher

Samuel Menashe

new and selected poems

christopher ricks editor

AMERICAN POETS PROJECT

THE LIBRARY OF AMERICA

Poems copyright © 1971, 1973, 1986, 2004, 2005 by Samuel Menashe. All rights reserved. Quotation from Stephen Spender, p xxi, reprinted with permission of *The New York Review of Books*, copyright © 1971 NYREV, Inc. Quotations from Donald Davie, p xxii, published by permission of the National Poetry Foundation; p. xx, from *The Poet in the Imaginary Museum: Essays of Two Decades* (Manchester, England: Carcanet Press, Ltd.). Copyright © 1977 by Donald Davie.

The paper used in this publication meets the minimum requirements of the American National Standard for Information Sciences—Permanence of Paper for Printed Library Materials, ANSI Z39.48—1984.

Design by Chip Kidd and Mark Melnick.
Frontispiece: © 1960 Richard M. Gummere

Library of Congress Cataloging-in-Publication Data:
Menashe, Samuel, 1925–
    [Poems. Selections]
    New and selected poems / Samuel Menashe ; Christopher Ricks, editor.
        p. cm. — (American poets project ; 17)
    Includes index.
    ISBN 1–931082–85–5 (alk. paper)
    I. Ricks, Christopher B. II. Title. III. Series.

PS3563.E47A6 2005
811'.54— dc22

                                                            2005044161

10 9 8 7 6 5 4 3 2 1

Samuel
Menashe

CONTENTS

GIVING THE DAY ITS DUE

Samuel Menashe

Of late, that old man's expression "in my day" surfaces when I look back at my life. In my day I knew of no poetry workshop except for one in Iowa—not that I ever thought of attending it. After World War II, I was in Paris under the G.I. Bill. I had been an infantryman in France, Belgium—the Battle of the Bulge—and Germany. At twenty-two I had a glamorous image of myself as a writer. Since I was fluent in French and Spanish, I would be a foreign correspondent, but at the Paris office of *The New York Herald Tribune*, I was told that hundreds knew these languages. Serbo-Croatian was needed.

I never expected to meet a poet, let alone become one. Poets were dead immortals, some of whose poems I knew by heart. I was writing short stories evoking my childhood or the War. One night in February 1949, I woke up in the middle of the night and there was the first line of a poem, entirely unforeseen. Had someone told me when I went to bed that night that this would happen, I would not have believed it. It was not that I did not "give myself permission" to be a poet—to use a phrase now prevalent. I just did not aspire to that exalted state. Moreover, how can one *decide* to be a poet? Here is my first poem, never published:

All my life when I woke up at night
There was darkness in a room
And quickly I must sleep . . .
Now I have found a bed beneath a window—
No purpose in this place—
By an unpatterned hazard of neglect, and yet
In its crossing of my ordinary fate
It is among stars that I awake

In 1950 I presented a thesis at the Sorbonne called *Un essai sur l'éxperience poetique* (*étude introspective*). By poetic experience, I meant that awareness which is the source of poetry. I had been a biochemistry major before enlisting. Although I was well read for my age, the only literary influences on my work so far as I can tell were the short poems of William Blake and the English translation of the Hebrew Bible. "The still small voice" of Elijah was my article of faith.

Upon my return from France, I looked into little and literary magazines, but I found nothing in them that corresponded to what I was doing. Although a few poems were accepted—the first by *The Yale Review*—I could not find a publisher for a book. Kathleen Raine came to mind because she was a Blake scholar. Thanks to her, my first book was published in London in 1961. She wrote the Foreword. Despite favorable reviews by Donald Davie, P. N. Furbank and others, I still could not find a publisher in New York, my native city, until 1971. October House was a small firm, few people knew the name. In London I was published by the well-known Victor Gollancz Ltd.

Those who approve of my poems call them economical or concise; the others dismiss them as slight. When the Beat poets "made the scene," I heard the pious platitude that it was good for poetry, but it was not good for my poetry. If confessional poetry was to the fore, I had nothing to offer its devotees. The only award or grant ever given to me was for a war story I wrote when I was thirty. Nevertheless, how many poets still alive were praised by Austin Clarke in *The Irish Times* (1961), where Derek Mahon reviewed my poems in 1987? My good fortune in England and Ireland seems miraculous to me. Although I was published by Penguin UK in 1996, I could not find a publisher in New York for my next book.

When I read a good short story I feel like an addict must feel when he gets a fix, but my poems do not tell stories. I never wrote a sonnet, yet in a way the poems are formal and they rhyme. Rhyme seems natural to me. There is a lot of rhyme, unnoticed, in ordinary speech.

At my age, more than ever, one thinks of death. Of course, as a survivor of an infantry company, I was marked by death for life when I was nineteen. In the first years after the war, I thought each day was the last day. I was amazed by the aplomb of those who spoke of what they would do next summer. Later, each day was the only day. Usually, I could give the day its due, live in the present, but I had no foresight for a future. Perhaps it is why I am still in the flat to which I moved when I was thirty-one years old:

AT A STANDSTILL

That statue, that cast
Of my solitude
Has found its niche
In this kitchen
Where I do not eat
Where the bathtub stands
Upon cat feet—
I did not advance
I cannot retreat

Metre, 2000

THE POETS ON
SAMUEL MENASHE

"To judge of poets is only the faculty of poets; and not of all poets, but the best." —*Ben Jonson*

Those of us who are not poets might remonstrate mildly, but we know what Ben Jonson means. Samuel Menashe is a true poet, and the poets have tested this claim and attested to its truth. Robert Graves welcomed him in person and welcomed his art highly, impersonally. Kathleen Raine introduced the poems to their first, their British, audience, in 1961, by way of a thought sown in Menashe's own manner: "In a treeless waste a seed is better than a pebble." Austin Clarke promptly alerted Irish readers to this American poetry, evoking "its suggestion of mysterious meaning" and its "axiomatic or imaginative effect." More than thirty years later, Derek Mahon paid tribute to a world of "concentration and crystallisation," an achievement that "opposes a tiny light to the vast orthodoxy." Rachel Hadas and Dana Gioia are among the other poets who have testified—in terms terse and laconic—to an art that earns those epithets. Of the poets' extended appreciations of this poet, those by Donald Davie, by Stephen Spender, and then again by Davie are excerpted here.

DONALD DAVIE
(1970)

One trouble is that his poems are as far from being traditional as they are from being in the fashion, or in any of the several fashions that have come and gone, whether in British or American poetry, over the last twenty-five or for that matter one hundred years. When Menashe himself is asked what tradition he thinks he is writing in, he is embarrassed and bewildered. Partly the question baffles him because the terms in which he thinks of his writing, and of writings by others, are not literary at all but as it were liturgical. And in the second place his linguistic situation is peculiar: his native tongue was Yiddish, though he was speaking English by the time he was five, and French (a language which ever since has meant much to him) by the time he was eleven.

On the other hand, though Menashe's attitude to poetry is thus un-literary, it is very insistently *linguistic*; his liturgical or devotional intent is directed to releasing the worshipful potentialities of *language*, most often of single words placed so as to draw out the full meaning locked in their etymologies—etymologies for which he has a very sure nose indeed, being aware through his Yiddish of the Germanic root of many English words, and through his French of the Romance derivations and kinships in others.

The most masterly poem along these lines is a recent one, "The Niche":

> The niche narrows
> Hones one thin
> Until his bones
> Disclose him

For here the two chains of intertwined assonance ("niche, thin, un*til*, his, him" spliced into "narro*ws*, hones, bones, disclose") only point up a surprising rhyme as it were in sense as well as sound; "disclose," the one word in the poem whose first syllable chimes with the "his" sequence as its second does with the "bones," has a meaning that is itself "disclosed" (unclosed, opened up) as the poem unfolds or flowers towards it. And of course it is all true; the meaning of a word is disclosed to us as we narrow it down.

(*The Poet in the Imaginary Museum*, 1977)

STEPHEN SPENDER
(1971)

Samuel Menashe is a poet of entirely Jewish consciousness, though on a scale almost minuscule. He is not one of the prophets, concerned with exodus, exile, and lamentation: but he is certainly a witness to the sacredness of the nation in all circumstances in life and in death. His poetry constantly reminds me of some kind of Biblical instrument—tabor or jubal—and the note it strikes is always positive and even joyous. His scale is, I repeat, very small, but he can compress an attitude to life that has an immense history into three lines.

One might of course regard Samuel Menashe as a survivor. He certainly knows all about fire and brimstone and underworlds.

Nothing seems more remarkable about him than that his poetry goes so little remarked. Here is a poet who compresses thoughts and sensations into language intense and clear as diamonds and no one walking through New York streets seems to wish to chalk up on a wall—among so many things they do chalk up:

Streets at night like decks
With spars overhead
Whose rigging ropes
Stars into scope

The best of writing a review is that sometimes one can persuade someone to read something. I hope, as a result of this, a lot of people will read Menashe.

(*The New York Review of Books*, 22 July 1971)

DONALD DAVIE
(*1986*)

Charles Olson, in a famous essay which codified what he called Projective Verse, insisted that the unit which the good verse-writer works with isn't the verse-line, isn't the word, isn't the metrical "foot," *but the syllable*. When Olson read his own poetry aloud, did his way of reading reflect this conviction of his? I don't know, for I never heard him read. The one and only style of reading that I know of, which forces the reader to attend to each and every syllable in what he hears, is the reading-style of Samuel Menashe, who for all I know has never read the Olson essay.

The niche narrows
Hones one thin
Until his bones
Disclose him

This, a complete poem, is not the sort of thing that usually came to us under the banner of Projective Verse. But hearing Menashe read it—eleven words, fourteen syllables —is to understand what it means in practice for a poet to compose by the syllable. The voice is enviably rich in timbre and resonance, but what matters is that it is exactly controlled. To get this poem over to an audience, bringing out how every syllable is irreplaceable in sound as well as sense, means slowing down the delivery of each sound far beyond what we are used to. Yet the accomplishment of Menashe as a reader is that he holds fast, through all these necessary retardations, to the shape of a conversational utterance, of something one might *say*, of (as Wordsworth said) "a man talking to men." Hearing it read by Menashe is an experience unlike any other known to me; when the poem has been performed, one has the illusion (and perhaps it isn't illusory after all) of having heard a very long poem indeed, and a very elaborate one.

A poet I know has said to me, admiringly and I think with a sort of shame, that the discipline of Menashe's always very short poems is "punitive." But Menashe doesn't mean to punish either himself or his readers; his poems have to be compact and close because only in that way can English words—*any* English word, if the right tight context be found for it—show up as worshipful, as having a wisdom and an emotional force beyond what we can bring out of it when we make it serve our usual occasions. It is easiest to see this when Menashe makes play with meanings locked into idiomatic expressions that we use unthinkingly. For instance, "follow your nose"—a common expression that Menashe as a Jew, his Jewishness sealed into his physiognomy, makes composed and witty play with. Or consider "elbow-room":

WINDOWS: OLD WIDOW

There is a pillow
On the window sill—
Her elbow room—
In the twin window
Enclosed by a grill
Plants in pots bloom
On the window sill

The pillow on the window sill is there for the widow's elbows to rest on it as she looks out into the street; that is elbow room in a literal way we had not envisaged. And in the twin window are the plants that bloom in a pot analogous to the widow, exposing her perhaps fading bloom to the street? Or are they not, since "Enclosed by a grill," an image of how shut up and shut off she is, capable of displaying her liveliness, and registering the liveliness of the street, only through a narrow aperture? Every window is a window-box, whenever it frames a human face looking out. But no answers are expected, or possible; simply, how much human pathos is compacted in the common expression "elbow-room" if only we will stay with it, dwell on it, convert it into an image!

This is an urban snapshot. And indeed the scene of Menashe's poems is nearly always that of cold-water apartments in old and run-down districts of Manhattan. But for those who have no particular attachment to that or similar environments, the poems have still the absorbing interest of pressing to the logical limit certain speculations and problems of modern poetics—an accomplishment the more remarkable since the poet shows no sign of having interested himself in such matters or in poetic theory generally. He is not a "primitive," but it will do no harm to read him as if he were. That way, one sees how seemingly abstruse considerations about how poetic language works are tied up with compassion for human suffering, and respect for human dignity.

(Foreword to Menashe's *Collected Poems*, 1986)

INTRODUCTION

Write short sentences: the old voice of authority, enjoining young people who are about to take exams. *Write short poems:* the still small voice that came to Samuel Menashe when young, heeded still in this, the year in which he turns eighty. His still small voice carries. It carries weight. The poems, in the terms of precise praise with which Dr. Samuel Johnson honored a seventeenth-century master who is now neglected (Sir John Denham), "convey much meaning in few words, and exhibit the sentiment with more weight than bulk." The poems have a way of pondering weight.

White hair does not weigh

> more than the black
> which it displaces—
> Upon any fine day
> I jump these traces

A pure Menashen poem, not least in its doing so much with what is in the least. Characteristic—in so many respectfulnesses—of the art of the man. Courage in age.

The poem is characteristic, first, in the imaginative aptness with which it arrives at the first of its endings:

"White hair does not weigh" is positioned with the end there, as though suspended weightlessly, or all-but-weightlessly, in the face of space. Characteristic, secondly, in its moving so lightly in and out of rhyme. There is the strong germane chime of *displaces / traces*, with the later word displacing the earlier one (even while preserving the traces of it). And then there is the ensuing assonance encompassing *day* as at once a rhyming and unrhyming word. Unrhyming if the poem were to be a quatrain, but rhyming as soon as, at its head, "White hair does not weigh" is seen to weigh as a line of the poem: *weigh / day*. (With *black* alone left then unrhyming—darkly?)

Yet although the poem is characteristic in being so succinct (tucked up like a garment, girded, the better to move with style and grace, girt for jumping traces, say), this is a poem at the same time freshly *un*typical. For elsewhere Menashe seldom avails himself of this particular turn by which a run of words that had at first been offered as a title is then found to convert itself—to divert itself—into becoming the first line of a poem proper. The title can be felt to flow on (white hair can flow, you know) into the first line, so is that then the second line? We weigh the likelihoods.

And then there are the other respects in which the poem is its own man. I think of the firm tact with which the matter of weight then jockeys honorably for position: "does not weigh more" canters through to the equestrian "I jump these traces," whereupon *traces* tucks up into itself (traces within itself) the thought of *races*. Some such combination of the bodily and the buoyant is just what a rider needs to weigh up. The happy levity is there in the way in which the phrase "jump the traces"—though not at all violent, unlike kicking over the traces—exults in a sudden release from restraint, from discipline. Yet within the poem, nothing could be less like jumping the traces: Menashe's lines are firmly in place, supple in their leatherliness, lithely together.

The discipline is characteristically loving (as discipline does well to be in horsemanship), and—as often in Menashe's sense of life—the love is to be felt in the way in which what might have been a dark or even malign thought is redeemed into a bright benign one. *One fine day:* how often this phrase harbors no good, refuses to glow but glowers instead in a vengeful resentment ("often used derisively with reference to the occurrence of some unlooked for event," warns the dictionary). *One fine day he'll learn his lesson.* Menashe's "any fine day" will not have any of this. His lessons amount to much more.

He remains, in his own way, weighty at eighty, but time and again (a phrase that brings to him, and thereby to us, pleasure), there is this teasing of levity against gravity. One of the many aspects in which the poems are entirely without snobbery is their delighting in commonplaces. Within these personable poems, a rueful resilience attends upon clichés. In one poem, your *level best* can be the opposite of a falling short—given their equanimity, the words can be a way of leveling with others and with yourself. Do you find yourself *saddled* with something?—but this is just what a rider sits in need of. What is *overlooked* may be being graciously surveyed, far from ignored. To *come to grief* may, on occasion, be a means of coming to one's senses, to a salutary sense of life's sad dignity. *The living end* may be a shouldering, not a shuddering. *Up in arms* is just what a baby should be. And *save your breath* may inspire a warmth of feeling that is far from the usual curt admonition, even while the frosty sensation is acknowledged as all too often the case. Menashe can make even *I told you so* an unexpected benison. Bless me.

Life is brought to the poems, and then brought back from the poems (regularly, not routinely), by courtesy of these phrases that could so easily have been left for dead. All those casualnesses that have become reduced to casualties: just think of them. (Instead of employing them unthinkingly.) For the poet can rescue these daily domestic servants from servility and from servitude. A. E. Housman, another poet whose poems are of the simplest and of the most mysterious, once remarked how difficult it is to write poems in praise of Liberty:

> There is a lack of detail about Liberty, and she has indeed no positive quality at all. Liberty consists in the absence of obstructions; it is merely a preliminary to activities whose character it does not determine; and to write poems about Liberty is very much as if one should write an Ode to Elbow-room or a panegyric on space of three dimensions.
>
> ("Swinburne," 1910)

It was left to Samuel Menashe to write, well, not an *Ode* to Elbow-room, but a hymn to it. "Windows: Old Widow" opens with a setting and a settling:

> There is a pillow
> On the window sill—
> Her elbow room—

It is Donald Davie who has understood this poem for us most exquisitely: see, above, "The Poets on Samuel Menashe."

An Ode to Elbow-room? Come to that, Menashe is not above writing a panegyric on space of three dimensions. The space would be diminutive, the dimensions capacious.

Perhaps the most pleasing, the most endearing, of these affectionate roundings upon the commonplace is

Menashe's play with *as you please*, which ceases to be the usual reluctant concession that is coldly calculated to bring a conversation to an end. Within Menashe, "as you please" is both *in whatever way pleases you*, and *given that you do so please the rest of us*. Or there is his related pleasure in "to whom I please":

> I left my seed in a grove so deep
> The sun does not reach through the trees
> Now I am wed to the wood and lord of all leaves
> And I can give the green blessing to whom I please

True, the world will sometimes stand in need of a very different impulse, an impulse that is not from a vernal wood (for there is a time to bless and a time to curse), but how lovely that there can still be poems of such entirety, giving no more and no less than their green blessing. What could easily have been the wrong kind of lordliness (the "lord of all leaves" lording it over all and sundry) finds itself blessed instead with a tone of well-grounded rights: "to whom I please," a turn of phrase that perfectly balances one's pleasing oneself and one's pleasing others. For "to whom I *choose*" would have offered quite other choices.

The poem's peace of mind is further to be felt in the way in which a particular kind of rhyme is rescued from its propensity to skewer askew: the para-rhyme, the rotatory rhyme that for Wilfred Owen, there in the "Strange Meeting" that was the Great War, can be heard to realize the stations of his military cross. For Owen's para-rhymes trek from progress, *escaped* to *scooped*, then *groined* to *ground*, then *bestirred* to *stared*, then *eyes* to *bless* (no green blessing there), then *hall* to *Hell*. . . . What a relief it is to meet, in the peaceful world of Menashe, "Now I am wed to the wood." For here is a rotation that is not despair turning away but is hope turning to. No longer is the para-rhyme para-military. Elsewhere in Menashe the device again breathes peace, in the moment when *hill* turns lovingly to *holy*, or *heels* to *hills*, or—at one point—*stored* to *star*.

All of which still leaves the critical questions about this poet as the manifest unmisgiving ones. What kind of poems are these? What, if anything, protects them from lapsing from the laconic into the perfunctory? What, if anything, makes it possible for them to achieve so many things, such a sense of being at one and the same time centripetally singular and centrifugally plural? If the poems never do feel exclusive in their appeal (their appeal to readers and to all the other powers that be), how do the actively imaginative principles of exclusion allow the poems to be at once sharply focused and rangingly speculative, so pared and all?

What kind of poems? Well (well and good), short poems. Agreed. These are short poems that are not—the critics have rightly insisted—epigrams exactly, or (rather) are exactly not epigrams. A different kind of wit is at work. Or aphorisms, really. A different kind of wisdom is at work. Yet these are poems that do belong within wisdom literature, that of the Psalms, say, or of Blake's shorter poems (Menashe often offering moreover not Proverbs of Hell but Proverbs of Heaven). Apophthegms, I'd say. Menashe, who relishes the shorter forms of things (including words), would be likely to prefer the form *apothegm*. Here is one such, one of Menashe's best and best-known:

> A pot poured out
> Fulfills its spout

Child's play? Just try it. A minimalist's maxim, the poem fulfills itself, just so. How perfectly the verb "fulfills" fulfills the promise of the generous thought. A promise, a mission, an obligation, a nature: these are the kinds of things that it is possible and desirable to *fulfill*. This is an author who is in awe of "the author of peace and lover of concord, in knowledge of whom standeth our eternal life, whose service is perfect freedom."

But where exactly does it emanate from, this sense that the poem, too, is no less full for being so happy to give itself entirely away?

At which point, one might extend Donald Davie's magnanimous sequence of thought. When attending to Menashe's poems, Davie found himself descending the scale of units, from verse-line to word to foot to syllable . . . Why not then to the very letter? For Menashe has something of Lucretius's cosmic comic pleasure in the thought that the atoms that constitute all that is physical are also the letters that constitute all that is verbal: *elementa*. Menashe's art pours together the elementary and the elemental. See how the word *pot* pours itself out into "**po**ured o**ut**." See how, fulfilled but not done with, the word is poured forth again: *pot* living again within "s**po**ut." But these are not the only fulfillments: how fluidly "out" is taken up, without damage or distortion, effortlessly, within "sp**out**." Not just *le mot juste* but *la lettre juste*. For Menashe (mindful that he is grateful to Britain for first publishing a book of his, as it had done for Robert Frost) has pointed out that his is precisely an American poem. British English, in adopting the spelling "fulfils," would forfeit the full acknowledgment of the word "fills" that American English proffers so calmly in "fulfills."

The poem is one of those kindly riddles that is so good as to let you in on the answer without delay. "What great poetry is not dramatic?" asked T. S. Eliot—or rather a speaker within a dialogue by T. S. Eliot. What great poetry is not riddling, might I ask?

Sometimes the riddling is more sly.

Autumn

I walk outside the stone wall
Looking into the park at night
As armed trees frisk a windfall
Down paths that lampposts light

Among the many things to be looked into in this poem
there is this one: a riddle to which one law-abiding answer
might be *copse*.

Or take (for it is generously offered) another such
poem, one that the British critic P. N. Furbank offered in
a 1961 review as brilliant, and that Barry Ahearn in 1996
unfolded in a sympathetically acute analysis of measure
and movement, right down to the rightness of the syllable
lengths. The poem has its sound effects, *sound* as trust-
worthy and as evoking the quiet sound in both senses of
that word.

A flock of little boats
Tethered to the shore
Drifts in still water
Prows dip, nibbling

The sketch has something of the comical levity-cum-
gravity of a Dufy, a seascape that then in this case enjoys
the further pleasure of teasingly forgoing, as Dufy does
not, all glamour of color. Simplicity, itself. And yet there is
so much that flocks into it, now that the little boats are
glimpsed, clearly, for this tender moment as a flock of
sheep. Altogether pacific.

The effect is all the happier because of the various
traditional thinkings that gather within such a figure of
speech. For instance, that (culturally or agriculturally)
there are elsewhere such things as *fields* of foam, or (more

muscularly) that one can *plough the waves*. Or that the sea itself has been unforgettably imagined as at once the force that grazes and what it grazes upon: "It is the unpastured sea hungering for calm" (the greatest line that Shelley ever wrote?). Or that the water is so fluid while the boats are so distinct (these flowings being alive within the sequence "Tethered to **the** shore," the tethered letters as crystals that dissolve). And, drifting there, in the immediate vicinity and not needing to be spelt out, there is a particular little word: *flotilla*. "A flock of little boats": f l o t i l l a, all undulating slightly, mildly jumbled, there to be nibbled at. A flotilla, a floating flock, fleetingly a fleet.

  Prows dip, nibbling

The sheep dip. This, not only as inclining their heads to nibble, but as the sheep dip: the preparation that healthily washes them down. The sheep dip and are dipped, cleanlily, by the still water.

  A countryman in George Eliot's *Middlemarch* was bantered for his pronunciation: "But he says, 'A ship's in the garden' instead of 'a sheep,' said Letty." A flock, a flotilla: Menashe's poem is altogether sheep-shape. And how precise of him to have come to eschew in revision the slackly-suggestive ellipsis that, in an earlier version of the poem, had taken an easier way out:

  Drifts in still water . . .
  Prows dip, nibbling

For what was waiting truly to be released was not stepping-stones:

  Drifts in still water . . .

—but space:

> Drifts in still water
> Prows dip, nibbling

Menashe is an unquenchable reviser, albeit one who is committed to quenching all such effects as he has come to find too palpable. His lines are there to be read between. Which means that above all they must not be underlined. And the ellipsis there in "Drifts in still water . . ." was a kind of underlining.

Menashe revises away.

> My mother was brought up on traditional poetry. Most of the poems she still knew by heart were much longer than mine. If I told her that I had revised a poem since my last visit, she would ask, "How much shorter is it?"

Whereas Whitman is forever expanding ("I shall be good health to you nevertheless"), Menashe contracts with us differently. He will be good health to us evertheless.

Nothing, then, is too small to matter. What difference might it make, for instance, to have a small word be no longer in italics? Once upon a time, a poem called "Inklings" ran like this:

> Inklings *sans* ink
> Cling to the dry
> Point of the pen
> Whose stem I mouth
> Not knowing when
> The truth will out

Now, in the present edition, the poem opens like this, at last, so that a slightly different truth will out:

> Inklings sans ink

The difference is in the respect in which (and with which) there is welcomed a strange eventful line from *As You Like It*. As You Please. A great many of Menashe's poems might be understood as *As I Like It*: in the way that I do, and given that I do, and (*sotto voce*) as I trust you will.

> Last scene of all,
> That ends this strange eventful history,
> Is second childishness, and mere oblivion,
> Sans teeth, sans eyes, sans taste, sans everything.
>
> (*As You Like It*, II.vii)

The earlier rendering in Menashe ("Inklings *sans* ink") might have left the impression—given the unmistakable allusion to Shakespeare (Shakespeare's teeth into Menashe's mouth)—that the playwright has the word "*sans*." He doesn't. He has "sans," there being in his time an English word that was perfectly happy to coexist as a French word. Times have changed, and with them, languages. The English language is now sans "sans." Menashe's line, so recently revised, registers the force of this recognition, this brief pang, that we are now without one good old way of saying without.

The effect is momentary, as so often in Menashe, but then again it is in touch with some cognate understandings: that though we have the momentaneous sense of "moment," we do have, too, the momentous one, and we are always within reach of yet another one that knows what momentum is. Menashe's poems are minute, and they may seem to last only a minute, but they have different kinds of moment. He comprehends not only "Spur of the Moment" but "The Moment of Your Death."

"Second childishness"? These poems are not afraid to be found childlike. For even while alive with tiny filaments, they have their sheer simplicity. This, while they are distinctly aware of all the things that threaten simplicity, or that simplicity may all too easily be demeaned into. In favor of simplicity as we often are, we need to be all the more vigilant that we not mistake for simplicity what is only simplistic, or simplified, or simple-minded, or (in the distinction invoked by Matthew Arnold) *simplesse*:

> When a genius essentially subtle, or a genius which, from whatever cause, is in its essence not truly and broadly simple, determines to be perfectly plain, determines not to admit a shade of subtlety or curiosity into its expression, it cannot even then attain real simplicity; it can only attain a semblance of simplicity. French criticism, richer in its vocabulary than ours, has invented a useful word to distinguish this semblance (often very beautiful and valuable) from the real quality. The real quality it calls *simplicité*, the semblance *simplesse*.
>
> (*On Translating Homer*, "Last Words," 1861)

For the real quality needs to know what it is up against. In the words of Arnold's reluctant heir, T. S. Eliot:

> Great simplicity is only won by an intense moment or by years of intelligent effort, or by both. It represents one of the most arduous conquests of the human spirit: the triumph of feeling and thought over the natural sin of language.
>
> (*The Athenaeum*, 11 April 1919)

The natural sin of language: something that is distinguishable from but not distinct from the original sin that infects even language.

The lapsed Protestant Samuel Beckett may have remembered the words of T. S. Eliot in 1919 ("It represents one of the most arduous conquests of the human spirit") in his 1931 book on Proust ("It represents a false movement of the spirit") when, in the very next paragraph, Beckett declared:

> The tragic figure represents the expiation of original sin, of the original and eternal sin of him and all his "socii malorum," the sin of having been born.

> > "Pues el delito mayor
> > Del hombre es haber nacido."

For man's greatest offense is that he has been born. The words of Calderon became the words of Schopenhauer and then the words of Joseph Conrad (as epigraph to *An Outcast of the Islands*) and then the words of Beckett. Samuel Beckett, meet Samuel Menashe:

> One weekend, walking with my father in Central Park, I said to him, "Your life seems like the expiation of a crime you do not even know you committed." At once he replied, "For the crime of having been born." My Catholic friends were pleased by this response. It proved—to them—the truth of the doctrine of original sin.

But then Menashe is not a "tragic figure," and his poems are not tragic figures of speech. His is the courage of comedy, flanked by the respect of innocence.

Peace

As I lie on the rock
With my eyes closed
Absorbed by the sun
A creak of oarlocks
Comes into the cove

Not just absorbing the sun, absorbed by it. No crick in the neck. Instead, a creak for the old cove, there in the (un-sounded) creek. Peace comes into its own.

Christopher Ricks
2005

Voyage

Water opens without end
At the bow of the ship
Rising to descend
Away from it

Days become one
I am who I was

Sheen

Sun splinters
In water's skin
Quivers hundreds
Of lines to rim
One radiance
You within

O Many Named Beloved
Listen to my praise
Various as the seasons
Different as the days
All my treasons cease
When I see your face

A-
round
my neck
an amu-
let
Be-
tween
my eyes
a star
A
ring
in my
nose
and a
gold
chain
to
Keep me
where
You
are
*

Roads run forever
Under feet forever
Falling away
Yet, it may happen that you
Come to the same place again
Stay! You could not do
Anything more certain—
Here you can wait forever
And rejoice at your arrival

Autumn

I walk outside the stone wall
Looking into the park at night
As armed trees frisk a windfall
Down paths that lampposts light

November

Now sing to tarnish and good weathering
A praise of wrinkles which sustain us
Savory as apples whose heaps in attics
Keep many alive through old winter wars

All my friends are homeless
They do not even have tents
Were I to seek a safe place
I would run nights lost
Ice pelting my face
Sent the wrong way
Whenever I ask—
Afraid to run back,
Each escape the last

Lie down below trees
Be your own guest
Give yourself up. . .
Under this attentive pine
Take your time at noon
The planes will drone by soon

Winter

I am entrenched
Against the snow,
Visor lowered
To blunt its blow

I am where I go

The Dead of Winter

In my coat I sit
At the window sill
Wintering with snow
That did not melt
It fell long ago
At night, by stealth
I was where I am
When the snow began

Warrior Wisdom

Do not scrutinize
A secret wound—
Avert your eyes—
Nothing's to be done
Where darkness lies
No light can come

I lie in snows
Drifted so high
No one knows
Where I lie

Between bare boughs
One star decrees
Winter clarity

January to July

January
Winter's bone
Gnawed, taunts
Dogs who hone
Jaws on bone
    February (Valentine)
Last year's rut
Stoned in mud
Bemoans my love
    March
Clay gapes
As rain pelts
Snow away
Ice melts
    April (Fool)
Stars I leap
Clearing a puddle
Why was I deep
In a muddle?
    May
A fanfare of ferns
Assembled upon air
Expands everywhere
    June
The glazed bay
Anchored hulls
Sky silvering
The cry of gulls
    July
Who would eat
An egg you fry
On the sidewalk,
In July?

Downpour

Windowed I observe
The waning snow
As rain unearths
That raw clay—
Adam's afterbirth—
No one escapes
I lie down, immerse
Myself in sleep
The windows weep

April

It is the sun that makes us smile
It is the sun and spring has come
Soon it will reach Norway
Her wooden villages wet
Laughter in each rivulet

Transfusion

Death awaited
In this room
Takes its time
I stand by
Your deathbed
Making it mine

The Moment of Your Death

My head bounces away
In the trough of a wave
You are unbound on your bed
Like water far from a shore
Nothing can reach you now
Not my kiss, not a sound
You are out of hearing
And I have run aground
Where gravel grinds
The face it blinds

The Bare Tree

My mother once said to me, "When one sees the tree in leaf, one thinks the beauty of the tree is in its leaves, and then one sees the bare tree."

1

Now dry stone holds
Your hopeful head
Your wise brown eyes
And precise nose

Your mouth is dead

2

The silence is vast
I am still and wander
Keeping you in mind
There is never enough
Time to know another

3

Root of my soul
Split the stone
That holds you—
Be overthrown
Tomb I own

4

Darkness stored
Becomes a star
At whose core
You, dead, are

5

I will make you a landscape
Spread forth as waves run

After your death I live
Become a flying fish

Pity us
By the sea
On the sands
So briefly

She who saw the moon last night
She who swayed with the chant
Died in her sleep or dreams—
To say she is dead seems scant.

Fall

Dry leaves fly
Down the stream
You walked by

Near the water
I want to die

The Host

I am haunted
Out of my house
Gaunt, dispossessed
By the homeless dead
These ghosts, guests
Have bled me white
No marrow is left
In the bone they bite

Grief

Disbelief
To begin with—
Later, grief
Taking root
Grapples me
Wherever I am
Branches ram
Me in my bed
You are dead

Epitaph

New deaths surround
Me step by step
Until I'm found
Engraved near you

One become two

Landmark

I look up to see
Your windows, the house
Standing on this street
Like an old tombstone
Whose dates disappear
I still name you here

I stood, I saw
The room you left
What you could see
The awe of death
Took hold of me

Still Life

Where she sits
With apples
On her lap
Kindling snaps
Into flame
What happens
Fits the frame

Triptych

When my mother
Was a young girl
Before the War
Reading sad books
By the river
Sometimes, she
Looked up, wisely
But did not dream
The day I would
Be born to her

She who is not
Who she was
Waits to be
Yet she is
Already
Mother
Whose child
Though not yet
Could not be
An other

All at once
I could see
My mother
In eternity
I told her
She always
Would be
The one
Whose son
You see

Life is immense
I said to her
Stirred some way
I could not say—
It is minute
She replied—
How we laughed
Though I had sighed

Enclosure

Hagia Sophia's high dome
Magnifies and confines
The mind's eye, home
Within oval lines

In Memoriam

1

You had your say
Said what you saw
That day I stood by
Your bed to draw you
Out of your silence
Your head in profile
Pillowed, your brow
Your unfailing eye

2

Now he lies dead
In a white shroud
Eons behind
His closed eyes
Bear him out

When my father was dying he said, "I feel receded into the distance . . . All of my life my spirit has been in a race with my body and now my spirit has overtaken my body."

The Offering

Flowers, not bread
Cast upon the water—
The dead outlast
Whatever we offer

Full Fathom Five

Each new death opens
Old graves and digs
My own grave deeper
The dead, unbound, rise
Wave after wave
I dive for pearls
That were his eyes
But touch bedrock—
Not a coral reef—
Where my father lies
I come to grief

Memento Mori

This skull instructs
Me now to probe
The socket bone
Around my eyes
To test the nose
Bone underlies
To hold my breath
To make no bones
About the dead

Forever and a Day

No more than that
Dead cat shall I
Escape the corpse
I kept in shape
For the day off
Immortals take

Family Plot

1

I know that grave
At a stone's throw,
A stone none throws,
That grave outgrown
Like a child's bed

2

When I was ten
My grandmother died
She was fifty-seven
I am fifty-five

The friends of my father
Stand like gnarled trees
Yet in their eyes I see
Spring's crinkled leaf

And thus, although one dies
With nothing to bequeath
We are left enough
Love to make us grieve

These stone steps
bevelled by feet
endear the dead
to me as I climb
them every night

Self Employed

Piling up the years
I awake in one place
And find the same face
Or counting the time
Since my parents died—
Certain less is left
Than was spent—
I am employed
Every morning
Whose ore I coin
Without knowing
How to join
Lid to coffer
Pillar to groin—
Each day hinges
On the same offer

In My Digs

Caked in a glass
That is clear
Yesterday's dregs
Tell me the past
Happened here

Curriculum Vitae

1

Scribe out of work
At a loss for words
Not his to begin with,
The man life passed by
Stands at the window
Biding his time

2

Time and again
And now once more
I climb these stairs
Unlock this door—
No name where I live
Alone in my lair
With one bone to pick
And no time to spare

At a Standstill

That statue, that cast
Of my solitude
Has found its niche
In this kitchen
Where I do not eat
Where the bathtub stands
Upon cat feet—
I did not advance
I cannot retreat

The Oracle

Feet east
Head west
Arms spread
North and south
He lies in bed
Intersected
At the mouth

Nightfall

Eye this sky
With the mind's eye
Where no light fades
Between the lines
You read at night
Binding that text
Which days divide

Morning

I wake and the sky
Is there, intact
The paper is white
The ink is black
My charmed life
Harms no one—
No wife, no son

On the Level

Does this desk, level
With the window sill,
Uphold my level best
Or is the bed better
For dreams that distill
Words to the letter

Tenement Spring

Blue month of May, make us
Light as laundry on lines
Wind we do not see, mind us
Early in the morning

Windows: Old Widow

There is a pillow
On the window sill—
Her elbow room—
In the twin window
Enclosed by a grill
Plants in pots bloom
On the window sill

Heat Wave

I catnap, wake
Naked on my bed
Scrap paper spreads—
Enough ink spilled
In rough drafts
To float the raft

Off the Wall

Broken mirror off the wall
All of a piece with the past
Whose splinters glint like glass
Stuck in the sole of my shoe—
If I'm out of luck
And down at the heel too
Are seven years enough
Time for me to do?

At Millay's Grave

Your ashes
In an urn
Buried here
Make me burn
For dear life
My candle
At one end—
Night outlasts
Wick and wax
Foe and friend

Le lac secret

They have now traced me to my uncles
One died a beggar in a room with no windows
And one danced until he was undone, like Don Juan
Though they try to find me out, I am still as the swan
While those who search grow grim
And darker in their doubt

Always
When I was a boy
I lost things—
I am still
Forgetful—
Yet I daresay
All will be found
One day

Take any man
Walking on a road
Alone in his coat
He is a world
No one knows
And to himself
Unknown

Yet, when he wanders most
It is his own way, certain
As spheres astronomers note
In their familiar motion

Telescoped

The dead preside
In the mind's eye
Whose lens time bends
For us to see them
As we see the light
Shed by dead stars
Telescopes enlarge

Twilight

Looking across
The water we are
Startled by a star—
It is not dark yet
The sun has just set

Looking across
The water we are
Alone as that star
That startled us,
And as far

Enlightenment

He walked in awe
In awe of light
At nightfall, not at dawn
Whatever he saw
Receding from sight
In the sky's afterglow
Was what he wanted
To see, to know

Old Mirror

In this glass oval
As love's own lake
I face myself, your son
Who looks like you—
Once we were two

Mirror Image

Ribs ripple skin
Up to the nipples—
Noah, equipped, knew
Every one has two—
This ark I am in
Embarks my twin

Pirate

Like a cliff
My brow hangs over
The cave of my eyes
My nose is the prow of a ship

I plunder the world

Infant, Old Man

Up in arms
That hold her high
Enough to bend
Her father's ear
She babbles by
Me on a bench
At my wit's end.

Paradise—After Giovanni di Paolo

Paradise is a grove
Where flower and fruit tree
Form oval petals and pears
And apples only fair . . .
Among these saunter saints
Who uphold one another
In sacred conversations
Shaping hands that come close
As the lilies at their knees
While seraphim burn
With the moment's breeze

Shade

Branches spoke
This cupola
Whose leaf inlay
Keeps the sun at bay

Just Now

With my head down
Bent to this pen
Which is my plow
I did not see
That little cloud
Above the field—
Unfurrowed brow,
You are its yield

Gray Boulder

Gray boulder
Beside the road
You devote me to age
Whose date none decodes
From signs of fire or ice—
Elephant among field mice
You crouched here alone
In the silence of stone

Adam Means Earth*

I am the man
Whose name is mud
But what's in a name
To shame one who knows
Mud does not stain
Clay he's made of
Dust Adam became—
The dust he was—
Was he his name

*From *Adamah*, 'earth' in Hebrew.

Leah bribed Jacob
With mandrake roots
To make him
Lie with her

Take my poems

Reeds Rise from Water

rippling under my eyes
Bulrushes tuft the shore

At every instant I expect
what is hidden everywhere

Paschal Wilderness

Blue funnels the sun
Each unhewn stone
Every derelict stem
Engenders Jerusalem

Manna

Open your mouth
To feed that flesh
Your teeth have bled
Tongue us out
Bone by bone
Do not allow
Man to be fed
By bread alone

'And He afflicted thee and suffered thee to hunger and
fed thee with manna, which thou knewest not neither did
thy fathers know, that He might make thee know that
man does not live by bread alone, but by every word that
proceeds from the mouth of the Lord does man live.'
—Deuteronomy VIII:3

Stone would be water
But it cannot undo
Its own hardness
Rocks might run
Wild as torrents
Plunged upon the sky
By cliffs none climb

Who makes fountains
Spring from flint
Who dares tell
One thirsting
There's a well

Promised Land

At the edge
Of a world
Beyond my eyes
Beautiful
I know Exile
Is always
Green with hope—
The river
We cannot cross
Flows forever

If I were as lean as I feel
Only my bones would show
Living bone, ideal—
Without a shadow—
For the exacting dance
That the Law commands
Until I overstepped
The forbidden ark
To take on flesh
Wrestling in the dark

The Shrine Whose Shape I Am

The shrine whose shape I am
Has a fringe of fire
Flames skirt my skin

There is no Jerusalem but this
Breathed in flesh by shameless love
Built high upon the tides of blood
I believe the Prophets and Blake
And like David I bless myself
With all my might

I know many hills were holy once
But now in the level lands to live
Zion ground down must become marrow
Thus in my bones I am the King's son
And through death's domain I go
Making my own procession

My angels are dark
They are slaves in the market
But I see how beautiful they are

As the tall, turbaned
Black, incense man
Passed the house
I called after him
And ran out to the street
Where at once we smiled
Seeing one another
And without a word
Like a sword that leaps from its lustrous sheath
He was swinging his lamp with abundant grace
To my head and to my heart and to my feet . . .
Self-imparted we swayed
Possessed by that One
Only the living praise

'The dead do not praise Thee.'—Psalm of David

The hill I see
Every day
Is holy

My Mother's Grave

Bones
Are mortar
For your wall

Jerusalem

Dust
Upholds
Your street

Dreaming

Windswept
as the sea
at whose ebb
I fell asleep,
dreams collect
in the shell
that is left,
perfecting it.

Hallelujah

Eyes open to praise
The play of light
Upon the ceiling—
While still abed raise
The roof this morning
Rejoice as you please
Your Maker who made
This day while you slept,
Who gives grace and ease,
Whose promise is kept.

'Let them sing for joy upon their beds.'—Psalm 149

The Annunciation

She bows her head
Submissive, yet
Her downcast glance
Asks the angel, "Why,
For this romance,
Do I qualify?"

The Abandoned One

A man awoke at dawn
After snow all night
Had hidden the town . . .
Nothing familiar was visible now
And in the world's white silence
His possessions became worthless
Yet he felt light and elated
Knowing he had nothing

From that day he gave
Himself to everyone
Like an orphan
In Babylon
Until he found his mother
And he knew he was her son
Naming her the Abandoned One

O Lady lonely as a stone—
Even here moss has grown

83

Sparrow

That busy body darts
Under the pigeon to filch
A crumb bigger than his bill
Beggar, thief, get what you can

He's no songbird—
Chirps one note—
There is a pearl
Stuck in his throat

The scrutiny
Of a chicken's eye
Terrifies me—
What does it think?
Not brain but beak
Chills my blood—
It stares to kill

Rural Sunrise

Furrows erupt
Like spokes of a wheel
From the hub of the sun—
The field is overrun—
No rut lies fallow
As shadows yield
Plow and bucket
Cart and barrow

Sudden Shadow

Crow I scorn you
Caw everywhere
You'll not subdue
This blue air

Awakening from Dreams

Flung inside out
The crammed mouth
Whose meal I am
Ground, devoured
I find myself now
Benignly empowered

The hollow of morning
Holds my soul still
As water in a jar

Norway

The way her blond hair hangs
Over the back of the chair
Reminds me of Norway
Where hay is racked
To hang that way—
Straight down—
On narrow fields
Flat as a board
Lapped between
Steep mountains
And deep fjords

I left my seed in a grove so deep
The sun does not reach through the trees
Now I am wed to the wood and lord of all leaves
And I can give the green blessing to whom I please

Pagan Poem

Widespread as the waves
Of the rising sea
Boughs begin to wave
Above me as I lie
At ease in the shade—
If I could make out
With one of these trees
I would take root here
Never to leave this grove
Where the wind weaves
In and out of boughs
Shining overhead—
I would break all vows
That bind me to your bed
If I could make out
With one pine instead

Fastness

I shoulder the slope
that holds me
up to the sun
with my heels
dug into dust
older than hills

Landscape

Boughs berserk
Spin one hill
Into space
Standing still
Olive trees race

On the field below
Moulded white oxen
Ponder each furrow
A man behind them
Cries *Via, Via*

Dusk

night
into
earth
from
rise
Voices

Pastoral

The neighboring hill
Where lambs graze
Lies ample and still
In its own haze

Moon Night

Old stones glow still on a path
Below the wall of the town
I see them and I love
Clear and whole
And so well
No ghosts
Groan at the gate
I am the tale they tell
Now without wind or word Know
This night is one and does not end
Only the daydreamers go

Ruins

Stone worn
Overgrown
Pristine thorns
Sheep shorn
Tinkling below
Roofless walls
Rooks overlook
I told you so
Babbles the brook

Old as the Hills

The lilt of a slope
Under the city
Flow of the land
With streets in tow
Where houses stand
Row upon row

Twilight Blues

(*Morton St. Pier*)

Lying here
Flat on my back
I can almost see
Myself in the morgue
On a slab, tagged

I am the corpse
No one will have
Not stabbed, stored
No one takes my life
It goes by the board

In Stride

Streets at night like decks
With spars overhead
Whose rigging ropes
Stars into scope

Night Walk

In eyes of strangers glimpsed
On the street at night
I see more than meets the eye
In the broad daylight

The circumspect passer-by
Keeps to himself, and yet
His eyes give him the lie
At once when they are met

Petals

In the shade below boughs
Which flowers overflow
Petals glow on the ground

Petals like snow
Drifting apart
Winter's sting
Is not as sharp.

Bearings

Now I hear nearby
That dog I heard last night
Barking at a distance
I have walked far enough
In the darkness to know—
Sometimes I ran—
How far I can go
To get where I am

The room of my friend
Is a violet chapel
Where in pale state he lies
And daydreams dapple
His blue eyes

Waterfall

Water falls
Apart in air
Hangs like hair
Light installs
Itself in strands
Of water falling
The cliff stands

A flock of little boats
Tethered to the shore
Drifts in still water
Prows dip, nibbling

Eaves at dusk
beckon us
to peace
whose house,
espoused,
we keep

Star-Crossed

This lunar air
Draws me to you,
The moon's magnet
Aligns that pair
Whom dragons slew,
Whose course was set
Before they knew

Western Wind

One hand cold
One hand hot
One turns pages
One does not
As I lie in bed
Reading poems . . .
Remembering how
You love this one
I've come to now
My arms are numb

The Sandpiper

The sandpiper
Scampers over sand
Advances, withdraws
As breakers disband

Each wave undergoes
The bead of his eye
He pecks what it tows
Keeps himself dry

On My Birthday

I swam in the sea our mother
Naked as the day I was born
Still fit at forty-four
Willing to live forever

Sketches: By the Sea

1

That black man running
Headlong on the beach
Throws back the white
Soles of his feet
Lightning strikes
Twice on the sand
Left foot and right,
My pen in hand

2

Hearing the sea
Not seeing it
On the other side
Of the dunes
Is enough for me
This morning
The distance I keep
From the sea I hear
Brings distance near

3

At night, off shore
Sometimes the lights
On the fishing boats
Sink out of sight
That string of lights
Salt water wets
Makes the fish rise
To tridents and nets

Dominion

Stare at the sea
you on your chair
sinking in sand,
Command the waves
to stand like cliffs,
Lift up your hand

So they stood
Upon ladders
With pruning hooks
Backs to the king
Who took his leave
Of gardening

This morning
I am forlorn
As he was then
No one born
After the war
Remembers when

Beachhead

The tide ebbs
From a helmet
Wet sand embeds

Passive Resistance

Step out of the line
You toe on gravel
At the castle gate
Whose crest consigns
Minions to death
For reasons of state
Whose secrets kept
Seal your own fate

Peaceful Purposes

Those flapping flags
That the wind cracks
Over the house
Like an attack
Might have been
Potato sacks
If dipped in
Another vat

Survival

I stand on this stump
To knock on wood
For the good I once
Misunderstood

Cut down, yes
But rooted still
What stumps compress
No axe can kill

White hair does not weigh

more than the black
which it displaces—
Upon any fine day
I jump these traces

Walking Stick

This stick springs
When you lean on it
It is still green
You can feel the sap
This stick gives
A spring to your walk
Old sticks snap
This stick bends like a bow
You are the arrow

To Open

Spokes slide
Upon a pole
Inside
The parasol

Scissors

Sharpen your wit—
Each half of it—
Before you shut
Scissors to cut

Shear skin deep
Underneath wool
Expose the sheep
Whose leg you pull

I am the hive
You inhabit
Celled inside
Me you multiply

Pan's work is done
When grown men
Become wanton
As children
Who leap and run
Through green country
Seizing all they see

Achilles

I am shocked
By skin that shows
Through a hole
In my sock

Shod I forgot
My heel is white
It does not bite

Lust puffs up
The Peacock—
Taut tail strut
Fan of Fire—
Lust
Shakes a Sire

A pot poured out
Fulfills its spout

Spur of the Moment

His head rears back
Cresting upon his neck
His uplifted legs prance
As he champs at the bit
The unbridled rider sits
With reins in hand
Astride this dance
He is saddled with

Simon Says

In a doorway
Staring at rain
Simple withstands
Time on his hands

Using the window ledge
As a shelf for books
Does them good—
Bindings are belts
To be undone,
Let the wind come—
Hard covers melt,
Welcome the sun—
An airing is enough
To spring the lines
Which type confines,
But for pages uncut
Rain is a must.

Peace

As I lie on the rock
With my eyes closed
Absorbed by the sun
A creak of oarlocks
Comes into the cove

The Reservoir

Sea gulls squawk
Over the water
We walk around
On your day off
Gaining ground
Before nightfall
Whitecaps squall
The walled water
Swallows the wall

Sheep Meadow

French spoken
across the snow
on Sheep Meadow
evokes a very rich hour
of the Duke of Berry . . .
three men traversing
a field of snow—
one of them alone—
hedged by trees
on the south side
where the towers
of the city rise . . .
one of those hours
in early afternoon
when nothing happens
but time makes room

Sunset, Central Park

A wall of windows
Ignited by the sun
Burns in one column
Of fire on the lake
Night follows day
As embers break

Carnival

Faces flowing up the street
Faces glowing to the feast
Great is the god they greet
Face to face, feet to feet

All Things That Heal

All things that heal
Salves, herb, balm
Goodness I feel
Established calm

What form is as fair
As sunlight in air
As poultice to skin
Thorns instantly tear

Night Music

(*pizzicato*)

Why am I so fond
Of the double bass
Of bull frogs
(Or do I hear the prongs
Of a tuning fork,
Not a bull fiddle)
Responding—
In perfect accord—
To one another
Across this pond
How does each frog know
He is not his brother
Which frog to follow
Who was his mother
(Or is it a jew's harp
I hear in the dark?)

Daily Bread

I knead the dough
Whose oven you stoke
We consume each loaf
Wrapped in smoke

Ghost at the Wake

For all I know
Of love and woe
My all and all
Forgoes no feast
Or show of grief
For me, his ghost
At this banquet—
He eats the most
And yet he weeps
For now he knows
I'm his, for keeps.

Another Song of Sixpence

The royal money is made of honey
Sunny is the Queen's face
For the counting house and parlor
Are one and the same place

And in the garden hanging golden clothes
Is the milkwhite Maid whose name is Rose
With so many birds singing by her hands
As the King silent at the window stands
While his Queen dreams on and smiles . . .
For black flies have become bees
And all dark weeds are flowers
And Afternoon is Endless
In the palace bowers

Infanta

Below, between
Her dam and her sire
She stands alone
In grown-up attire

Small Kingdom

In their doorways women sit sewing
By the good light of afternoon
And nothing is beyond knowing
Though the sun shall go down soon

A shepherdess near a bramble ditch
And the Princess in the Alcazar
Keep the same precise stitch
And they both can see far

And when the knell tolls
All are wondering who—
If it is a lady, many bells
For a beggar, one will do

Salt and Pepper

Here and there
White hairs appear
On my chest—
Age seasons me
Gives me zest—
I am a sage
In the making
Sprinkled, shaking

Family Silver

That spoon fell out
Of my mother's mouth
Before I was born,
But I was endowed
With a tuning fork

Improvidence

Owe, do not own
What you can borrow
Live on each loan
Forget tomorrow
Why not be in debt
To one who can give
You whatever you need
It is good to abet
Another's good deed

Dinner

The sparrow
His eye is on
Hops to crumbs
He comes by
One at a time
Shy of the sum
He needs to dine

At Cross Purposes

1

Is this writing mine
Whose name is this
Did I underline
What I was to miss?

2

An upheaval of leaves
Enlightens the tree
Rooted it receives
Gusts on a spree

3

Beauty makes me sad
Makes me grieve
I see what I must leave

4

Scaffold, gallows
Do whose will
Who hallows wood
To build, kill

5

Blind man, anvil
No hammer strikes
Your eyes are spikes

Fire Dance

Must smiles subside in a sigh
And sobs underlie laughter
Shall we always leap high
With flames leaping after

Cargo

Old wounds leave good hollows
Where one who goes can hold
Himself in ghostly embraces
Of former powers and graces
Whose domain no strife mars—
I am made whole by my scars
For whatever now displaces
Follows all that once was
And without loss stows
Me into my own spaces

Transplant

I would give
My liver, kidneys
Heart itself
For you to live
In perfect health
With me, your clone
Whose grafted cells
Grow marrow, bone

If all else fails
Do not reject
My skin or nails
Whatever's left
Of me for you
By a hair's breadth
Will see us through

The Living End

Before long the end
Of the beginning
Begins to bend
To the beginning
Of the end you live
With some misgivings
About what you did.

Night Watch

The heart I hear in bed tonight
Is mine—it frightens me
To hear my heart so clearly
It could stop at any time

Keep your ear to the ground
I was told without fear
Now I am hollowed for sound
And it is my heart I hear

Sleep

gives wood its grain
Dreams knot the wood

Dreams

What wires lay bare
For this short circuit
Which makes filaments flare—
Can any bulb resist
Sockets whose threads twist
As fast as they are spun—
Who conducts these visits
Swifter than an eclipse
When the moon is overcome?

Home Movie

Awake at once
No space between
The day and dream
Seen as it runs
Me off the screen
No time to splice
Slices of life—
I'm wide awake,
No second take.

Inklings

Inklings sans ink
Cling to the dry
Point of the pen
Whose stem I mouth
Not knowing when
The truth will out

What to Expect

At death's door
The end in sight
Is life, not death
Each breath you take
Is breathtaking

Save your breath
Does not apply—
You must die.

The Visitation

His body ahead
Of him on the bed
He faces his feet
Sees himself dead,
A corpse complete
With legs and chest
And belly between
Swelling the scene
Of the crime you left,
Taking your time,
Angel of Death

Red Glints in Black Hair

It is the rose below white
Gold suns under sea green
A nose formed for insight
Things visible but unseen
Keeping my eyes to the king
As I call wise night my queen

A Bronze Head

He's in his garden now
Sticking his neck out
Of a flower bed,
A head without shoulders

We are not statues yet
Nor about to become
Immortals, thoroughbreds
At the starting post
Programmed to run
A race against ghosts
Whose inside track
Stakes out the hindmost
For us, taken aback
By the prowess we lack.

Anonymous

Truth to tell,
Seldom told
Under oath,
We live lies
And grow old
Self disguised—
Who are you
I talk to?

Eyes

Eyes have their day
Before the tongue
That slips to say
What they see at once
Without word play,
Betraying no one

Be deaf, dumb, a dunce
With cleft palate
Bereft of speech
Open eyes possess
That wilderness
No tongue can breach

Awakening

Like one born again
To the same mother
I wake each morning
The same, another
Who takes my name
But cannot place me
In dreams, nightmares
Where I became
The one she bears

Someone Walked Over My Grave

The breath breaks a cold shuddered hollow
That instant, unbearably, I know
The beauty of this world

Those lips the young man my father
Found more fair than the bud of a rose
Now almost touched to dust—kiss that dust
You trod God of Life, God of the world

The Niche

The niche narrows
Hones one thin
Until his bones
Disclose him

Whose Name I Know

You whose name I know
As well as my own
You whose name I know
But not to tell
You whose name I know
Yet do not say
Even to myself—
You whose name I know
Know that I came
Here to name you
Whose name I know

The Sprite of Delight

The sprite of delight
Springs, summersaults
Vaults out of sight
Rising, self-spun
Weight overcome

The sea staves
Concave waves

Descent

My father drummed darkness
Through the underbrush
Until lightning struck

I take after him

Clouds crowd the sky
Around me as I run
Downhill on a high—
I am my mother's son
Born long ago
In the storm's eye

Commemoration

Old as I am
This candle I light
For you today
May be the last one
Of your afterlife
With me, your son—
With me you die twice.

Skull

Fingers spread to hold
The back of my head,
Thumbs at the neck probe
Skullbone hands enclose
Like a ball one throws
Or kicks as it rolls
Bouncing out of bounds—
Who knows on what grounds

Scribe, Condemned

Each *t* you cross
And *i* you dot
Decrees that loss
Shall be your lot

If you forgot
To blot the ink
Your bones will rot
Your flesh will shrink

"Make It New"

Scrap old texts,
Draw the line
No type sets,
Undermine
The alphabet,
Abet rhyme
Stanzas stress

Diner

Ghosts haunt their old haunts
But where will these ghosts go
Now that *Homer's* closed
And as for us
Who are almost ghosts
Where can we eat
With a garden view
And a bell tower
Across the street—
No place like *Homer's*

R and R

Regret
slips its noose
around the neck

Remorse
sinks its tooth
into the corpse

Heat Wave

Sheets entangle him
Naked on his bed
Like a toppled mast
Slack sails bedeck
At sea, no ballast
For that even keel
He cannot keep—
No steering wheel
As he falls asleep

Apotheosis

Taut with longing
You must become
The god you sought—
The only one

The stars are
Although I do not sing
About them—
The sky and the trees
Are indifferent
To whom they please
The rose is unmoved
By my nose
And the garland in your hair,
Although your eyes be lakes, dies

Why sigh for a star
Better bay at the moon
Better bay at the moon . . .
Oh moon, moon, moon

In the Ring

Knock yourself out
Shadowboxing—
Skull numb, mouth dry—
Blind the mind's eye

Rest in Peace

I stood my ground,
Clay underfoot,
Looked into the grave
They dug for you
Who left your bed
Unmade yesterday
To lie here, dead
With nothing to do—
The mourners fled

Captain, Captive

Captain, captive
Of your fate
Fast asleep
On the bed you made
Dream away
Wake up late

Rue

For what I did
And did not do
And do without
In my old age
Rue, not rage
Against that night
We go into,
Sets me straight
On what to do
Before I die—
Sit in the shade,
Look at the sky

Here

Ghost I house
In this old flat—
Your outpost—
My aftermath

Due soldi di speranza

I leave two pennies
On my table
To keep hope in sight

I enable myself
By any device
An angel would recognize

Even if he came
While I was away
A good sign
Might make him stay

INDEX

ABOUT THIS SERIES

The American Poets Project offers, for the first time in our history, a compact national library of American poetry. Selected and introduced by distinguished poets and scholars, elegant in design and textually authoritative, the series makes widely available the full scope of our poetic heritage.

For other titles in the American Poets Project, or for information on subscribing to the series, please visit: www.americanpoetsproject.org.

ABOUT THE PUBLISHER

The Library of America, a nonprofit publisher, is dedicated to preserving America's best and most significant writing in handsome, enduring volumes, featuring authoritative texts. For a free catalog, to subscribe to the series, or to learn how you can help support The Library's mission, please visit www.loa.org or write: The Library of America, 14 East 60th Street, New York, NY 10022.

AMERICAN POETS PROJECT